To Joan —
You are awesomee!.

Bri

perspectives
ON DESIGN
COLORADO

Published by

PANACHE
P A N A C H E   P A R T N E R S

Panache Partners, LLC
1424 Gables Court
Plano, TX 75075
469.246.6060
Fax: 469.246.6062
www.panache.com

Publishers: Brian G. Carabet and John A. Shand

Printed in Malaysia

Distributed by Independent Publishers Group
800.888.4741

PUBLISHER'S DATA

Perspectives on Design Colorado

Library of Congress Control Number: 2009939296

ISBN 13: 978-1-933415-59-8
ISBN 10: 1-933415-59-2

First Printing 2010

10 9 8 7 6 5 4 3 2 1

Right: Pinnacle Mountain Homes, page 49

Previous Page: Poss Architecture + Planning, page 59

Panache Partners, LLC, is dedicated to the restoration and conservation
of the environment. Our books are manufactured with strict adherence
to an environmental management system in accordance with ISO 14001
standards, including the use of paper from mills certified to derive their
products from well-managed forests. We are committed to continued
investigation of alternative paper products and environmentally
responsible manufacturing processes to ensure the preservation of our
fragile planet.

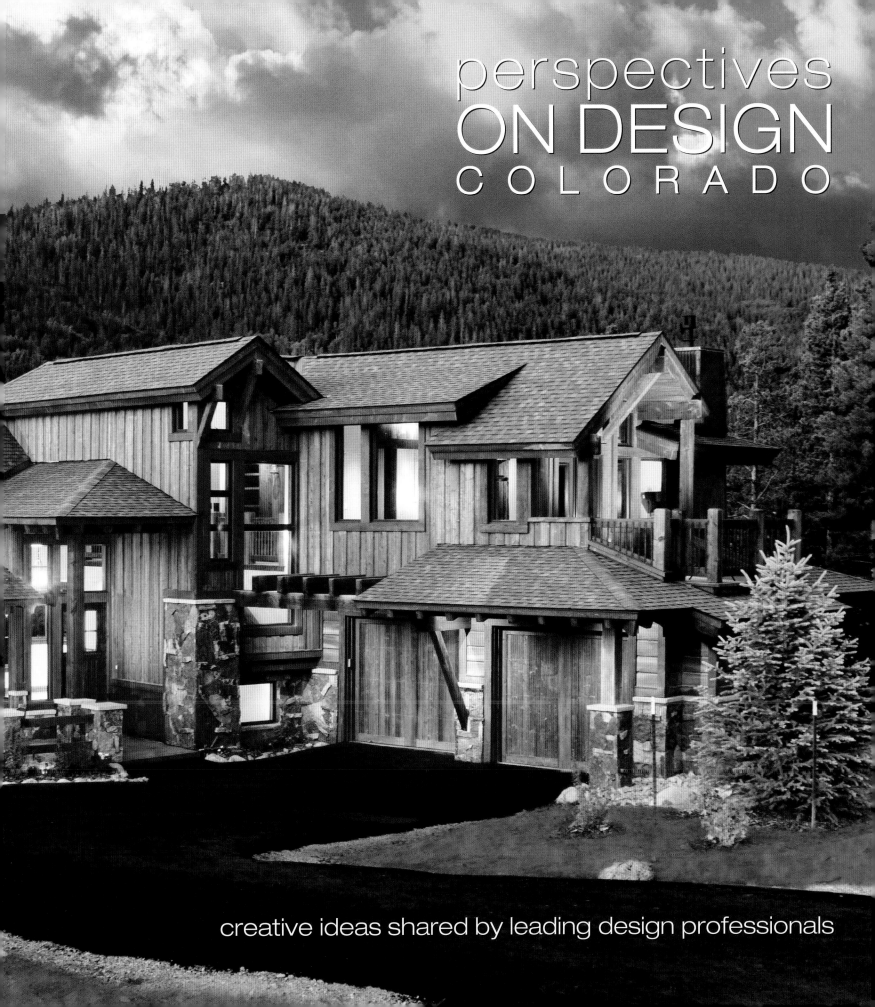

perspectives
ON DESIGN
COLORADO

creative ideas shared by leading design professionals

Sears Barrett Architects, page 69

introduction

Decorative Materials International, page 21

Spiro Lyon Glass, page 149

Creating the spaces in which we live and achieving the beauty we desire can be a daunting quest—a quest that is as diverse as each of our unique personalities. For some, it may be a serene, infinity-edge pool in the backyard; for others it may be an opulent marble entryway. Aspiring chefs may find a kitchen boasting the finest in technology their true sanctuary.

Perspectives on Design Colorado is a pictorial journey from conceptualizing your dream home to putting together the finishing touches, to creating an outdoor oasis. Alongside the phenomenal photography, you will have a rare insight into how these tastemakers achieve such works of art and be inspired by their personal perspectives on design.

Within these pages, the state's finest artisans share their wisdom, experience and talent. It is the collaboration between these visionaries and the outstanding pride and craftsmanship of the products showcased that together achieve the remarkable. Learn from leaders in the industry about the aesthetics of a finely crafted sofa, how appropriate lighting can dramatically change the appearance of a room, or what is necessary to create a state-of-the-art home theater.

Whether your dream is to have a new home or one that has been redesigned to suit your lifestyle, *Perspectives on Design Colorado* will be both an enjoyable journey and a source of motivation.

chapter one: concept + structure

Brikor Associates 19

Harrison Custom Builders 29

K.H. Webb Architects 39

Pinnacle Mountain Homes 49

Poss Architecture + Planning 59

Sears Barrett Architects 69

chapter two: elements of structure

In-Site Design Group 79

Decorative Materials International 91

Brown Dog Designs 103

Myers & Company Architectural Metals 109

Custom Edge Marble & Granite 115

contents

chapter three: elements of design

Sara Zook Designs 119

Interior Intuitions 131

Digital Media Innovations 143

Spiro Lyon Glass 149

Bob Levey Decorative Finishing 155

Denver Glass Interiors 159

Gallegos Corporation 163

chapter four: living the elements

Sones Landscape Architecture Group and MacDesign 167

Bluegreen 179

Gallegos Corporation 185

Sears Barrett Architects, page 69

Myers & Company Architectural Metals, page 109

"Design means making the impossible look simple."

—Greg Phare

Digital Media Innovations, page 143

Sones Landscape Architecture Group and MacDesign, page 167

"Architecture is a synthesis of connections with the environment, the person commissioning the home, the designers, and those implementing the construction."

—Bill Poss

Bluegreen, page 179

Gallegos Corporation, page 163

Foss Architecture + Planning, page 59

Denver Glass Interiors, page 159

Harrison Custom Builders, page 29

K.H. Webb Architects, page 39

Sones Landscape Architecture Group and MacDesign, page 167

Decorative Materials International, page 91

Brikor Associates, page 19

"You can't build anything without integrity."

—Gary Woodworth

Decorative Materials International, page 91

Bluegreen, page 179

In-Site Design Group, page 79

"Soon we will measure design quality with new criteria. A home's lightness, energy consumption, and sustainability will redefine the concept of beauty in architecture."

—Sears Barrett

Poss Architecture + Planning, page 59

K.H. Webb Architects, page 39

Sears Barrett Architects, page 69   K.H. Webb Architects, page 39   Brikor Associates, page 19

concept + structure

chapter one

Harrison Custom Builders, page 29

Poss Architecture + Planning, page 59

Pinnacle Mountain Homes, page 49

Surrounded by stunning views and thriving with worldwide influence, Aspen offers the ideal backdrop for custom homebuilding. And after working on the East Coast and across the country, the principals of Brikor Associates have established their firm in Aspen knowing that the setting is as close to perfect as possible. The city allows for high levels of creativity and attracts sophisticated homeowners from around the globe, giving Brikor Associates the ability to work with a variety of architects, artisans, and designers.

Named after its two founding members, Brikor Associates began in 1995 with a strong brother-and-sister team: Briston Peterson and Korba Andrews. Because their father was a developer, the two have a comprehensive understanding of the business and a deep-rooted appreciation for the industry; they know what it takes to make the process a success. Believing in word of mouth, Briston and Korba know that they're only as good as their last project and rely heavily on the quality of their work. Maintaining a mid-size boutique firm allows them to collaborate with the entire team and meet the high demands of Aspen homeowners. From custom tree houses to sprawling ski lodges, and everything in between, Brikor Associates creates homes that fit beautifully into the Colorado landscape with refinement and dedication.

"When the principals of a firm remain intimately involved in the process, both the home and its owners stand to benefit."

—Briston Peterson

BRIKOR ASSOCIATES

ABOVE & FACING PAGE: Located in Snowmass, a vacation home with ski access features stunning millwork throughout; trim details appear in the living room, dining room, and kitchen. Designed by Poss Architecture + Planning, the home won an AIA award for design and reveals strong craftsmanship.

PREVIOUS PAGES: We built a custom stairway that pulls the home's design elements together. Mahogany railing and recycled bamboo flooring complement features throughout the home and offer a warm palette. For the home's exterior, we used cedar, mahogany, and locally quarried Telluride gold. A zinc roof system plus Duratherm windows and doors add strength and longevity to the home's contemporary appeal.

Photographs by David Marlow

"Sophistication levels of homebuilding have changed; the standards continually rise. It's a challenge we enjoy meeting with each project."

—Korba Andrews

ABOVE: Set on a 100-acre parcel in Wildcat Ranch, an old ranch compound maintains its farmhouse feel after renovation. Hand-hewn, reclaimed siding and leveled moss rock give the exterior its distinct look. With weathering and age, the home's appearance improves—offering high comfort and low maintenance to the owners.

FACING PAGE: The owners wanted to keep the original integrity of the home and still have modern spaces, so we collaborated with Poss Architecture + Planning and put the idea of additive architecture to work. With this approach, the home maintains its original style and has the look of continuing additions.
Photographs by Wayne Thom

"When it comes to building a home, preparation is key. The happiest homeowners assemble their team early and know that experience is priceless."

—Briston Peterson

ABOVE & FACING PAGE: Teaming up with Studio B Architects, we blended the old with the new for a West End home in downtown Aspen. The main, modern portion of the home connects to an old miner's cottage with a loggia and features an outdoor kitchen, a Zen garden, and a soothing water feature with a bamboo spout. Preserving as much as possible, we kept the cottage's original windows and maintained its antiquated appeal.
Photographs courtesy of Studio B Architects

"The collaborative approach brings together a wide range of industry talent and expert insight. For the homeowner, the best way to nourish the process is to trust the professionals and take comfort in their proven knowledge."

—Korba Andrews

LEFT & FACING PAGE: The home features contemporary style with historic overlay, mimicking Victorian elements and traditional Colorado mining houses. Natural light floods the home's interior, which features stunning Aspen views.
Photographs courtesy of Studio B Architects

Whether working from detailed drawings or a quick conceptual sketch, Harrison Custom Builders has the savvy and creativity to bring the most complex of architectural details to fruition. And it's those masterful details that add up to timeless masterpieces. The dedicated Harrisons lead every project with craftspeople who have been on staff for decades and a whole cadre of trusted subcontractors, specialists, and sources; it's no wonder that the Cherry Hills Village builder has earned such acclaim.

Building on the legacy established by Aubrey Harrison in the 1950s, son Lynn and his wife, Pam, with their son Scott and his wife, Christie, along with Lynn's brother Rod, have an impressively diverse residential portfolio. Their open-book, cost-plus business model ensures that homeowners benefit from quality materials at the company's cost; their level of personal involvement makes the process easy and enjoyable; and their dedication means that every home created under the Harrison name is built to be enjoyed for generations. While creating timeless homes has been a constant throughout the firm's history, the Harrisons continue to evolve their homebuilding approach to include the most innovative and green features. They incorporate geothermal heating and cooling systems and photovoltaic arrays when possible and use energy-efficient materials across the board, resulting in substantially decreased energy consumption.

"It's imperative to work with only the best craftsmen. When plans called for a plaster ceiling, we didn't just find someone who knew how to work in plaster; we collaborated with an artisan who specializes in restoring plaster in state capitol buildings."

—Lynn Harrison

HARRISON CUSTOM BUILDERS

"Ingenuity and creativity make it possible to find the perfect equilibrium of old and new."

—Pam Harrison

ABOVE: Reclaimed materials are a wonderful way to create an instant sense of history but require a great deal of advanced planning and even more skill during the installation. Even when we use new materials, we custom cut and carefully place each element. For the French cottage-style home, we utilized reclaimed antique parquet from the Midwest, stone from France, and clay roof tiles from England.

FACING PAGE: For a couple who wanted the detailing of their English Tudor home to feel authentic, we meticulously crafted the windows, fireplace, and beamed ceiling with Gothic peaks. The home does, however, possess modern elements. The Tudor arch is a double-wall design, and electronic shades are concealed within to give a clean aesthetic. The mahogany cabinetry looks more like furniture than storage space. Completing the state-of-the-art-meets-Old World theme, the Venetian plaster ceiling features an up-lighting system.

PREVIOUS PAGES LEFT: The material palette and detailing are true to the home's English Tudor character. From the wood floors and paneling to the crown moulding and plaster ceiling, every design element is impeccable. Drawing from our extensive pool of resources, we had the limestone mantel hand-carved in Mexico; it's very high quality and far more cost-effective than importing such a piece from Europe.

PREVIOUS PAGES RIGHT: New homes should have an innate timelessness about them. Through our real estate brokerage company, we have had the pleasure of working with homeowners in acquiring the perfect site and then building their home with beautiful, lasting materials: limestone exterior and patios, Vermont slate roof, and copper gutters and downspouts; the interiors are equally well appointed.
Photographs by Ron Ruscio

ABOVE: Indeed, the beauty and durability of cut limestone is unmatched. The natural material was made to live outdoors, and when it's hand cut by a true artisan, like in the English Tudor estate, the stone's veining and artifacts can really be showcased. Over time, limestone weathers well and develops a wonderful patina.

FACING PAGE TOP: Wine cellars can have a cave-like ambience, but the homeowner wanted something more modern, so we combined mosaic flooring and ceiling brickwork with lightly stained alder trim and bold wrought-iron doors. The dramatic material palette gives the space a contemporary vibe. Eye-catching ceiling details are a theme throughout the home. The great room's ceiling is supported by trusses—structural beams that are also decorative. It takes skilled personnel and cranes to get architectural elements like this in place, and the challenge was magnified here because the beams had to go up at the framing stage and stay pristine throughout the construction process.

FACING PAGE BOTTOM: The best designs are site-specific. Adjacent to the Highline Canal, the property has a wonderful pastoral feel, so the European-inspired architecture feels right at home. The two-story residence is nestled into an equestrian site with established trees and affords the luxury of French doors and windows in the basement looking out onto open space. Kansas rubble limestone, Vermont slate, copper, and locally reclaimed brick make up the perfect material palette for the style and locale.
Photographs by Ron Ruscio

"When appropriately detailed, a new home with classical roots can look and feel like it has been standing for a hundred years."

—Scott Harrison

ABOVE: If you want a home to last more than a century and be virtually maintenance-free for the first few decades, going with solid, time-tested, natural materials is the only option. The French-inspired estate's slate roof, stone façade, and copper gutters, valleys, and flashings are essential to the home's durability. Elements like the porte cochère and imported French antique fountain add to its timelessness.

FACING PAGE TOP: Richly stained, quartersawn oak paneling and walnut flooring establish the formal English Tudor environment. The geometric ceiling detail seems like it's right out of the '20s and is a welcome yet unexpected touch.

FACING PAGE BOTTOM: We've had a lot of experience incorporating antique elements into new construction; it requires planning, patience, and sometimes a bit of improvisation. Imported from Portugal, the pantry doors inspired the kitchen's casual French countryside look, which is furthered by the traditional apothecary drawers and farmhouse sink. Our talented woodworkers and painters brought the look together in the blue-grey and brown cabinetry. A delightful paradox, modern organization elements are concealed behind the authentic European pantry doors.

Photographs by Ron Ruscio

"Attention to detail is the secret to building architecture with instant authenticity."

—Christie Harrison

ABOVE: Site planning is critical in determining the right footprint of the home and orienting it to the views, as the resort-like backyard so eloquently demonstrates. Each piece of Indiana limestone was hand-cut for a specific part of the exterior and precisely numbered for a seamless installation process. The water feature with dramatic fire element looks as though it flows down into the basement, but it's really recycling back up. The placement is perfect for enjoyment within the home, on the terrace, or in the adjacent swimming pool.

FACING PAGE TOP: We excavated about 40 feet out from the house and incorporated massive retaining walls to give the basement mountain views and an entertaining terrace. The room's scale is matched by uplit coffers with a generously tall ceiling.

FACING PAGE BOTTOM LEFT: The home looks historical but it's actually a well-detailed new construction. We stayed true to the theme of the home in our refined material palette.

FACING PAGE BOTTOM RIGHT: In the second-floor master bedroom, we created an English Tudor look through the beamed ceiling and preserved the ambience with a roll-down painting that hides the flat-screen television.
Photographs by Ron Ruscio

Magnificent in setting, design, and energy—one owner of a K.H. Webb Architects home said it best, but the sentiment applies to the firm's whole portfolio of residential creations. Based in the memorable mountain town of Vail, the firm has been translating people's stylistic penchants and lifestyle needs into three-dimensional works of art since the late '90s.

Kyle Webb, the firm's founding principal, has strategically surrounded himself with a diverse team of professionals; their unique educational backgrounds, methodologies, and aesthetics come together to enrich each project and push the traditional boundaries of design. Undertaking projects from master planning to design consultation but specializing in architecture—both new construction and renovation—the boutique firm has earned a solid reputation for innovative designs that perfectly embody the personalities of their inhabitants, the timeless beauty of the land, and the rich character of the community.

"The most successful residential projects are those in which the prospective homeowners are regarded as integral members of the design team."

—Kyle Webb

K.H. WEBB ARCHITECTS

ABOVE & PREVIOUS PAGES: As with any project that has more than one owner guiding its creative direction, there's a large amount of diversity in not only the homebuilding process, but also the end result. When one person wants a contemporary home and the other has more traditional tastes, we have to work from these basic ideas and allow a completely distinct style to evolve—one that results in a home where both spouses feel comfortable. Set in Vail Valley, this home is quite contemporary with a rustic flair. To achieve this delicate balance, the house utilizes a variety of textures: traditional siding, barn wood, stone, and copper. The interior acknowledges a more contemporary side, with functionality being a top priority such as in the Bulthaup kitchen. By raising the cooking space and shielding it from the dining table, dinner guests aren't distracted by any kitchen activity, but those who are preparing the meal don't feel disconnected from the rest of the party either.

FACING PAGE: My clients wanted Hollywood to meet the mountains. And with a soaring stone fireplace, which connects to both the indoor and outdoor living spaces, we achieved a very elegant interpretation of their requests.
Photographs by Gibeon Photography

"Maximizing the site's features and the locale's resources is a common-sense approach to architecture, but it's an approach that demonstrates environmental stewardship and sensitivity to the project's monetary parameters."

—Kyle Webb

RIGHT: From the outdoor terrace, the homeowners can see Gore Creek. Since the home was set on a very tight, restricted lot that falls steeply down toward the creek, we worked closely with the landscape architect to create some great outdoor spaces. The terraces have heaters and beautiful furniture, and they progress in series down a path that connects to the water.
Photograph by Gibeon Photography

LEFT: Natural light cascades into the voluminous space to enhance the warmth of the stone and wood details. Because entryways establish the architectural tone, it's important that they make a memorable statement.
Photograph by Kimberly Gavin Photography

FACING PAGE: A veritable bachelor pad set in Vail, the home has an urban loft ambience, which we achieved through a diverse palette of mountain materials. The see-through fireplace is a steel box; we chose steel stairs, beams, and columns, too. To bring some warmth into the home, we combined this cooler material with a generous grouping of cherry and maple woods.
Photograph by Dreamcatcher Imaging

"Sustainable design should be organically woven into the design process, not tacked on to be trendy."

—Kyle Webb

ABOVE: The exterior façade is a contemporary interpretation of a more traditional aesthetic, and thus it melds well with the other homes in the Beaver Creek ski resort area. The homeowner, being a devoted modern art collector, wanted a place that could meet his progressive aesthetic preferences and also display his art pieces— so the interior is quite contemporary with plenty of clean, white spaces.
Photograph by Todd Winslow Pierce

FACING PAGE: The front transitions quests through an arrival sequence from the courtyard to the living room with a 40-foot ceiling. With this intricate ceiling work, we were looking for a historical illusion that could fit into a traditional subdivision. It was inspired by the Timberline Lodge in Oregon, and the timber frame works well as a complement to the homeowner's art collection.
Photographs by Dann Coffey

Entering the construction industry from a background in finance and technology—and after years of management consulting and running his own internet company—Chris Renner is not your typical builder. But a lifelong passion for architecture always lingered. Soon he was able to capture that dream by founding Pinnacle Mountain Homes, a custom homebuilding company that thrives on Chris' management skills. By streamlining the homebuilding process, Pinnacle Mountain Homes manages to capitalize on his greatest strengths: organizing time and organizing money. This white-collar approach has created one of Colorado's most interesting and successful residential portfolios.

As both a relative outsider and newcomer to the building world, Pinnacle Mountain Homes has employed this approach with stellar results—boasting that every one of its homeowners is a reference. And Colorado seems the perfect place, for here the need for fascinating mountain homes beckons the talent of such a great construction company. Functioning as consultant to architects and homeowners alike, the company continues to redefine what good homebuilding is all about.

"The custom homebuilding process can be complex and daunting, but with the right approach, it's not only painless but actually enjoyable."

—Chris Renner

PINNACLE MOUNTAIN HOMES

"The right materials always elevate the project."

—Chris Renner

ABOVE: We believe in working smarter, not harder, as our most important role is played out during the design phase—before construction ever begins. Thoughtful planning not only produces higher finishes, but enables us to deliver at a lower cost.

Photograph by Jeff Scroggins, jeffscroggins.com

FACING & PREVIOUS PAGES: Colorado's mountain homes need to exude warmth, and as with many of our custom homes, lighting takes center stage in the great room. The custom wine closet exemplifies creative use of space—it had to be in the open, had to fit in with the aesthetics of the room, and had to be temperature controlled at 58 degrees year-round.

Facing page photographs by Jeff Scroggins, jeffscroggins.com
Previous pages photograph by Bob Winsett

"It's amazing what an impact the process of building has on the design."

—Chris Renner

RIGHT: Multiple gables define the mountain home, a concept that nestles the home into its landscape. Indigenous wood and stone run throughout, and large expanses of glass help to blur the line between interior and exterior.
Photograph by Jeff Scroggins, jeffscroggins.com

"Blueprints only go so far—never underestimate the value of an artistic builder."

—Chris Renner

RIGHT & FACING PAGE: So many decisions are actually made in the field that we have to be entirely mindful of the creative, artistic vision. The details are not necessarily in the blueprints, so experience must dictate the proper approach. Here, various artistic touches on the ceiling, corbels, and radius staircase create a manageable scale and add subtle artistry to the smallest of details.
Photographs by Jeff Scroggins, jeffscroggins.com

"Turning concepts into reality—nothing could be more fulfilling."

—Chris Renner

ABOVE & FACING PAGE: Not everything has to be over the top, even in the most luxurious of homes. Unlimited budgets are easy; projects that require value with limited resources are the exciting ones. Most of our time is spent discovering how to maximize the components of a build. This involves taking key spaces, such as kitchens and dining rooms, and elevating them to a higher status. This ability to holistically envision the entire process has really driven our custom-homebuilding journey.

Above photograph by Bob Winsett

Facing page top left photograph by Chris Renner

Facing page top right and bottom photographs by Jeff Scroggins, jeffscroggins.com

Commissioned for projects as far away as Russia and throughout North America, Poss Architecture + Planning has mastered the art of designing architecture that at once captures the essence of its locale and echoes the lifestyle of the people who interact with it. International ventures provide plenty of opportunities for creative problem solving, yet the firm's leadership admits that projects close to Poss' headquarters in Aspen and Carbondale are personal favorites because there's something profoundly rewarding about enhancing your own region's architectural fabric.

The firm is comprised of dozens of creative and talented architects and has a special interior design division, ensuring that every work of architecture is cohesively conceptualized and realized. These professionals embrace the values and collaborative culture established by founding principal Bill Poss more than three decades ago. Known for their deft ability to capture the essence of mountain and resort lifestyle in projects ranging from private residences to luxury hotels to community planning ventures, the architects and designers of Poss take visions beyond the expected with utmost sensitivity to the environment.

"Architecture is a synthesis of connections with the environment, the person commissioning the home, the designers, and those implementing the construction."

—Bill Poss

POSS ARCHITECTURE + PLANNING

"Good design considers the tiniest of details, engages all the senses, and presents artful compositions at every turn."

—Andy Wisnoski

ABOVE & FACING PAGE: We oriented the home to take full advantage of the Roaring Fork Valley views; the home has a long and lean footprint, and while it nestles into the landscape with a low profile, the interior feels quite spacious. Significant overhangs protect the south-facing walls of glass from the sunlight's intensity and add to the architectural character.
Photographs by David O. Marlow

PREVIOUS PAGES: Transparent bridges connect the architecture with nature and link the home's four wings: main living spaces, master suite, guestrooms, and guest common areas. Designed for privacy, functionality, and site maximization, the plan is a refreshing departure from conventional mountain lodges; similarly, glass and steel are incorporated into the traditional palette of wood and stone for a distinct stylistic statement. For visual and aural pleasure, Bluegreen, the landscape architect, created a water feature that meanders around and through the site. Another key organizing element is the Montana granite, which runs through the home from the entryway, subliminally enticing guests deeper into the main living spaces.
Photographs by Pat Sudmeier

"It's incumbent on all of us to make a difference in the way we build."

—Bill Poss

RIGHT: Designed expressly for its steeply sloped site, the home at once embraces and erases the traditional concept of mountain living. Site constraints led us to organize the home around a central courtyard and sculpture garden; pocketing glass doors offer the epitome of indoor-outdoor living in the warmer months and a strong connection with nature even in the middle of winter. The juxtaposition of Kasota stone and metal elements is a pleasant counterpoint to the strong roof lines, which echo the mountains' drama.

Photograph by David O. Marlow

"Lifestyle, aspirations, aesthetic preferences, and connection to the land—all of these elements must be thoughtfully considered."

—Bill Poss

ABOVE & RIGHT: Accomplishing disparate goals with a single structure takes creative planning. In Telluride, we created a home that, from a distance, reads as a collection of established ranch structures with traditional forms, reclaimed wood, and a patinaed metal roof; it seems to have evolved over time, and it's hard to imagine the site without it. Up close, however, the home reveals itself as a delightfully reinterpreted composition—something new, modern, welcoming. The home enjoys panoramic views of the landscape and wildlife—elk routinely visit the property.

Above photograph by David O. Marlow
Right photograph by Pat Sudmeier

FACING PAGE: The dramatic Aspen Mountain home is decidedly contemporary yet clearly alludes to historical forms. Its multilevel plan allows for ski-in access and makes it easy for the homeowners to welcome family and friends for extended stays or weekend getaways. Including half-intervals, the home boasts seven levels connected by a central stairway. The unique site and the area's history as a mining hub drove the home's design and inspired us to select materials like local red sandstone, Douglas fir, and copper.

Photographs by Pat Sudmeier

"As architects, we have been entrusted with a great responsibility for the infringements—the buildings—on the land. It's a responsibility not to be taken lightly."

—Bill Pollock

ABOVE & FACING PAGE: Given an incredible site with 360-degree views, we could have done virtually anything with the design aesthetic; but taking cues from the client, we gave the mountain home a distinct contemporary flavor. The homeowner originally lived next door—in a home that we remodeled several years ago—and when he had the opportunity to purchase his neighbor's property, we were commissioned for the new primary residence. Sites with great views in the Aspen area are generally on challenging topography, and this one was no different. We used the tight, steep, triangular lot at the base of Smuggler Mountain to our advantage, and the home seems effortlessly integrated into the mountainside. From the master suite level on top to the car collector's dream garage on the lowest level, the home's programming and circulation feel logical, natural. Bluegreen's collaboration on the landscape design really accentuates the home's welcoming character and indoor-outdoor appeal. Though floor-to-ceiling glass doors that retract to a 12-foot opening are certainly memorable, the main living area is perhaps the most breathtaking place in the home. It is enclosed by three walls of glass that create what the homeowner describes as "a reverse snow-globe effect"—day, night, summer, winter, the vistas of Aspen are spectacular.

Photographs by Jason Dewey

The range of architectural styles and innovative ideas evident in Sears Barrett Architects' work seems too broad to come from one firm. Few architects have the perspective Sears has gleaned from experiences across a wide social spectrum and a background that includes fine art, construction, and the latest concepts in solar and sustainable design.

In the late 1970s, as energy-saving concepts were gaining traction, Sears' interest in solar design inspired him to create one of the first design-build firms specializing in passive solar residences. His earth-integrated, passive solar homes soon caught the attention of the Solar Energy Research Institute—now the National Renewable Energy Institute—based in Golden, where he joined the staff to create and manage research programs gauging the performance of passive solar designs.

In 1984, Sears opened his architectural firm with the goal of melding the technical lessons he had learned working at SERI with an aesthetic of elegant, site-sensitive design to serve residential clients. In the decades since, he and his staff of architects have built a reputation for originality and a willingness to embrace the stylistic tastes of the high-end homeowner, be the home European, traditional, mountain rustic, or urban contemporary.

"Soon we will measure design quality with new criteria. A home's lightness, energy consumption, and sustainability will redefine the concept of beauty in architecture."

—Sears Barrett

SEARS BARRETT ARCHITECTS

"Residential architecture is a search for the perfect fit, for what best suits the site, the clients' lifestyles, and their aesthetic goals. There is a true sense of delight when a design finds that harmony."

—Sears Barrett

ABOVE: Designed for an established in-town neighborhood, the home's courtyard design marries timeless materials to a contemporary plan. The blue-grey slate roof floats above a window and soffit system of clear Douglas fir. Hand-shaped, Texas cream limestone clads the entire exterior. In an effort to open the interior to the forested one-acre site, the courtyard side of the house is framed entirely in glass. Custom Anigre doors and cabinets with minimal flush detailing throughout lend a warm and elegant feel to the interiors.

FACING PAGE: The garden is just as important as the interior spaces of the house. A water element flows among the large limestone boulders to create a focal point within the landscaping. Unique to the home's design is its orientation toward the garden and the diverse canopy of deciduous trees. The living, dining, and family rooms as well as the kitchen overlook the forested yards of neighboring homes, giving the illusion of acres of urban woodlands.

PREVIOUS PAGES: Although the house has large overhangs, the stone columns were designed to guide the eye beyond the light wood wall and structures. At almost any point on the grounds, there is evidence of how the home was built with respect to the existing site—the architecture seems to bend and turn with the trees.

Photographs by Ron Ruscio

"We are intrigued by courtyards wrapped within the walls of a home, which can offer the perfect balance of tranquility and refuge."

—Sears Barrett

ABOVE: To infuse the home with the ambience of a classic Italian villa, the material selection was crucial. We developed carved limestone detailing for all the arches and columns to contrast with the rustic Kansas sandstone walls.

FACING PAGE: An extensive loggia wraps across the main floor of the house, from the family room to the master bedroom, serving as a layered outdoor space that shelters the house from the intense sunlight. Custom trim and plaster work in the kitchen and living room ceilings lend the home a sense of Venetian refinement. The homeowners were integrally involved. In fact, the owner's wife and friends spent weeks meticulously hand-painting every plaster medallion on the kitchen ceiling. There are imported limestone fireplaces and hand-carved mahogany doors—even the mantels were handmade for the house. When entertaining, the homeowners often set up lights over the descending terraces, creating the feel of a piazza in Italy.
Photographs by Ron Ruscio

"In really successful projects, the energy of collaboration is in full play. Great designs result from a unified vision initiated by the owner and the architect, which is then elevated by the contributions of the interior and landscape designers. You can really feel it when everyone is aligned."

—Sears Barrett

ABOVE: Upon first surveying the two-acre site, we realized that half of it was completely bare due to years of use as a horse pasture; the other half wasn't any more impressive with its sparse pine trees and small ranch house. Our approach was to design the house with the mature existing pine trees acting as the fourth wall of a courtyard. We placed an elaborate pond and waterfall at the center of the courtyard, framed by three walls of French doors.

FACING PAGE: As one moves through the house, the waterfalls and pond are engaged from every room. Prairie-style, four-foot overhangs give a real emphasis on the horizontal—even the bedrooms on the upper floor have balconies with large overhangs to provide shelter from the sun. The master bedroom provides a serene two-chambered suite with uplit pyramidal ceilings. Arranged to provide an engaging setting, the study offers an ideal spot for conversation or reading by the fire.
Photographs by Ron Ruscio

"Green is no longer just a color to homebuyers. It's a mark of awareness—a direct reflection of their conscientious effort to build sensibly upon the earth."

—Sears Barrett

ABOVE: Blessed with a captivating view over 20 miles of the Black Forest to Pikes Peak, the 50-foot curved wall of glass spans the open plan from the great room to the contemporary kitchen.

FACING PAGE: Simplicity in form and refinement of detail were the primary aesthetic goals in the foothills residence. Through expression of individual rooms as distinct forms on the exterior, the scale of the home was reduced. The powder room continues the warm neutral color scheme with an inventive use of bamboo reed panels, simple millwork, and inlaid tile.
Photographs by Tim Maloney

"Urban interior design should never compete with spectacular city views. Good design should complement the setting."

—Judy Gubner

elements of structure

chapter two

Innovative. Incisive. Involved. These are words that describe Judy Gubner and Colleen Johnson's work ethic as they engage in each new project at their dynamic interior design firm: In-Site Design Group. Since 1992, the talented team has been commissioned to conceptualize and create designs for ultra-luxury residential interiors across the United States.

In-Site's philosophy focuses on partnership and passionate dedication to excellence. The designers excel in every phase of interior development, collaborating closely with owner, architect, and contractor to achieve the optimal execution of the creative vision. The firm has been lauded by homeowners and the design industry for its inventive artistic skills, business acumen, and impeccable service. Judy and Colleen accept only those projects that they can personally design and manage to provide the utmost attention. Presentations of ideas and solutions facilitate well-informed decision-making while demystifying the creative journey. Documentation of design details is compiled in a project book replete with elevations, specifications, tear sheets, floorplans, and samples, so homeowners have a complete record of their choices and know exactly what to expect. The adept duo are members of the American Society of Interior Designers and are Certified Aging in Place Specialists. Moreover, they are approachable and accountable, a powerful creative force resulting in distinctive interiors that reflect elite homeowners.

IN-SITE DESIGN GROUP

ABOVE & FACING PAGE: Our design for a new, exclusive downtown condominium in Texas complements the strict architecture through use of contemporary furnishings and an unexpected color scheme. Used primarily for business trips and meetings, the home's clean and precise environment features crisp edges, polished granite, and black leather. We injected the rooms with lightness and humor through brightly hued accents. Three spots of color are repeated throughout the home, bringing the space to life. We designed custom rugs for the living room, dining room, family room, and study; each has lines running from one to another in perfect micro-precision.

Photographs by Jason Jung, Estetico

PREVIOUS PAGES: We revitalized an urban high-rise space by introducing new interior architectural elements. A textural, metalwork fireplace surround is a sleek focal point, and hand-painted and mocha-glazed millwork creates a warm, inviting environment. The monochromatic color palette and furnishings are subdued, allowing the exciting 360-degree city views to shine.

Photograph by Scott Hasson, Hasson Photography

"Designers are arbiters of taste and must work to reflect the homeowner's lifestyle through a shared aesthetic vision."

—Colleen Johnson

ABOVE & FACING PAGE TOP: We believe that great interior design is about the homeowner's preferences, lifestyle, and dreams. Comfortable working in all genres, we designed a gracious Colorado mountain home with a heightened sense of refinement by incorporating furnishings with a distinctly European flair. Our work is meant to express originality using principles of interior design: judicious use of color, materials, exquisite architectural elements, furnishings, and fine art. We call upon our established resources, expert fabricators, and artisans for such customized details. Our inlaid yew and walnut table with complementary buffet pairs with custom-designed rugs and accent pieces to provide a graceful but updated elegance to the dining room and great room.
Photographs by Jason Jung, Estetico

FACING PAGE BOTTOM LEFT: We created a warm and inviting living room in this faithful reproduction of a territorial-style home.
Photograph by Greg Hursley

FACING PAGE BOTTOM RIGHT: We created a French chateau spirit in the home's anteroom, which leads to the wine cellar. We incorporated stone accents, old beams, and custom ironwork to frame charming trompe l'oeil murals of family members on a classic French vineyard for a delightful tasting-room ambience.
Photograph by Jason Jung, Estetico

"Universal design focuses on creating easy and equitable access for all. There are many subtle elements involved in designing an interior to accommodate special needs, and all can be beautiful."

—Judy Gubner

ABOVE: The classical bath is lined in honed limestone. We had an original mosaic commissioned based on an Italian painter's ethereal work to add a glorious art wall above the spa tub. Our sophisticated bathroom design is an Italian-Asian fusion of elements; the Sumi glass door and windows allow soft, glowing light into the space for a feeling of serenity.

FACING PAGE: Architectural groundwork must be laid first. We work to support the architectural premise with color, texture, and furniture to create a cohesive feeling. The kitchen remodel required wall removal to open up the space from its original 1980s', dated, small-room layout. Bamboo flooring, concrete counters that resemble supple leather, a custom pole-mounted rotating television, and cabinets made of rift-sawn white oak with Sumi glass panels create a fresh, easy-living design.
Photographs by Jason Jung, Estetico

"Artistic vision and sophisticated organizational skills are required to go from concept to completion."

—Colleen Johnson

LEFT & FACING PAGE: Flowing communication is essential to a successful project. The vision can only come together in a perfect solution when there is synergy. In a prestigious Palm Springs community we created distinct areas but tied them together very strongly through the use of color and pattern. The deep coral tones of the landscape are pulled into our interior design, reminiscent of 1940s' Old Hollywood glamour. Genuine Venetian plaster walls have a subtle sheen, and custom walnut parquet flooring is hand-distressed and laid in a beautiful pattern. Crocodile embossed leather tables add richness. Stenciling on ceilings and custom rugs share scrollwork designs to unify the rooms in an understated, elegant way.

Photographs by Jason Jung, Estetico

"Attention to detail to the point of micro-precision is essential when designing small spaces."

—Judy Gubner

ABOVE LEFT: The bamboo staircase sports leather treads with subtle Sumi glass panels. Metal handrails wrapped in woven leather provide a manly grip. The bamboo flooring is a sustainable element. We love designing with tile, stone, metal, and wood: Décor is simply the icing on the cake.
Photograph by Jason Jung, Estetico

ABOVE RIGHT: A gentleman's master bath features varied materials. The tri-toned limestone floor adds subtle texture and interest. The adjoining custom closet has transparent glass panels for a fresh look, and rift-cut white oak cabinetry is echoed in the unique wood vanity basin and sconce lighting.
Photograph by Jason Jung, Estetico

FACING PAGE: Working closely with the Gulfstream engineers and design team, we created the sophisticated interior for a new G-V transatlantic jet, where every inch of space was considered. We selected materials to meet stringent safety codes and ensure ease of maintenance. Our custom carpeting, divan-style sofa, passenger chairs, and cockpit interior feature shades of blue with copper accents. Woven leather side panels, exotic wood tables and veneered privacy walls exude elegance, and multiple television screens are integrated throughout the aircraft to provide the ultimate in luxury travel.
Photograph by Eric Currey, Tecmap Corporation

Decorative Materials International

Aspen, Colorado — Denver, Colorado — Vail, Colorado

"There's definitely a romantic quality to salvaging beautiful tile and stone. You wonder where each piece has come from—someone's house, a church, another mosaic—and appreciate the history, the mystery."

—Margot Hampleman

ABOVE: I've always loved tile and stone, and it's been wonderfully rewarding to bring together cottage industries across the country in a showroom for the public and the trade. It's not just a showroom, though—I have relationships with these artists, artisans, and specialty importers. My design team and I enjoy helping people realize their visions through our resources—materials and people alike. The custom mosaic is the perfect example of a timeless design presented in a trendsetting way. Half a dozen different types of stone comprise the piece: Gold, white, and pale yellows form the field, while deep golds and black create the pattern. It's the subtle variety of limestone and marble that makes the design so stunning.
Photograph courtesy of Artistic Tile

FACING PAGE: People don't necessarily think of stone and tile as being environmentally friendly materials, but when you can give new life to materials in buildings that are no longer in use, it's the most green thing you can do, really. We sourced antique French terracotta for the floors and had the backsplash made in Italy from recycled stones including precious blue lapis. The countertop is a slab of limestone from Israel; it will soak up the natural stains of oil and wine and, like in France, be seen as a mark of culinary artistry.
Photograph courtesy of Decorative Materials

"Art Nouveau, Old World, Arts-and-Crafts, Contemporary? I love them all, really. It's about finding the right style for the people and the place."

—Margot Hampleman

ABOVE & FACING PAGE: Whether the desired look is contemporary or rooted in tradition, there's a type of stone or tile that's perfect for the project. It's just a matter of identifying the right application—a floor clad in large textural pieces or a wall with a memorable design motif. For the green bathroom, we orchestrated a hand-painted mural on honed marble: The look is entirely custom, yet the monetary investment is only a fraction of a comparable mosaic piece; the border adds a little bit of pizzazz and unifies the space. In the modern powder room, three-dimensional blue limestone clads the walls in 24-inch-square pieces, creating interesting tonality and depth. The crisp look of the brushed stainless vanity and acrylic matte sink perfectly complements the natural stone.
Photographs courtesy of Decorative Materials

"Mosaics don't adorn the wall, they become the wall."

—Margot Hampleman

TOP RIGHT: Huge porcelain tiles, 24 by 48 inches, prove that you can't have too much of a really good thing. The squiggle pattern glazed onto the tiles has a striking and dramatic repetition and is exactly what the sophisticated space needed.
Photograph © Florim/Casa dolce casa, all rights reserved

BOTTOM RIGHT: You can do so much with a monochromatic scheme. Dark blue tessera at the base of the modern shower blend into pale blues at the top for an artistic, interesting effect. When we receive a design like this from an artisan, it comes in precisely labeled sections for seamless installation—it's like the artisan is on-site.
Photograph courtesy of Bisazza

FACING PAGE LEFT: For a contemporary look, we recommend a simple material palette like the one used in the shower. The smoothness of the grey-and-white planked marble on the walls and ceiling is punctuated by tumbled pebbles underfoot.
Photograph courtesy of Artistic Tile

FACING PAGE RIGHT: The Art Nouveau Bisazza design called for a spectacular silver and gold leaf glass mosaic design. The look is a fresh interpretation of transitional European design.
Photograph courtesy of Ingrid Fretheim Interiors

"The beauty of centuries-old mosaic floors—their natural patina and undulation—can be translated into modern designs through the talents of stone artists."

—Margot Hampleman

ABOVE LEFT & RIGHT: Three-dimensional projects are tricky—the design, manufacturing, and installation require an artistic approach. In the fireplace mantel, surround, and hearth, handmade ceramic tiles meet ornate architectural elements. The Oregon-based artist who created the ensemble practices a proprietary glazing process that involves many layers and multiple firings for a complex and inimitable aesthetic.
Photographs courtesy of Encore

FACING PAGE LEFT: Natural stone from all over the world—Colombia, the Middle East, and elsewhere—makes a huge impact in the small space. The iron aspen leaf mirror and cast concrete sink with metal base and copper faucet complete the room.
Photograph courtesy of Decorative Materials

FACING PAGE RIGHT: Castle Interiors' design of the nature-inspired bathing area called for a complex material palette, namely the intricate mosaic on the walls, bench, and floor. The bamboo-inspired mosaic of honed and polished verde luna and Emperador dark creates a unique experience.
Photograph courtesy of Castle Interiors

"One trip to Europe and you'll understand why no work of architecture, grandiose or quaint, is complete without tile or stone designs."

—Margot Hampleman

RIGHT: Waterjetted stone is a brilliant alternative to wallpaper because the aesthetic is exquisite and the application is appropriate even in moist areas like kitchens and baths. Our vanity design perfectly complements the stone mural.
Photograph courtesy of Decorative Materials

FACING PAGE: Classic tones of black, grey, and white offer infinite possibilities, and they're appropriate for settings of any style, from ultra-modern to fabulously traditional. Art glass is shiny, eye-catching, low-maintenance, and can be cut into all sorts of shapes—from strips to curves.
Photographs courtesy of Mixed Up Mosaics and New Ravenna

"Mosaics are quite possibly the most eternal of artistic expressions."

—Margot Hampleman

TOP LEFT: The tree mural is made of 24-by-48-inch porcelain that has been glazed and fired to reveal a beautifully understated shimmer.
Photograph © Florim/Casa dolce casa, all rights reserved

BOTTOM LEFT: Collected from nature and then sorted by size and color, the pebbles and stones that form the garden's planters are extremely popular because of their versatility.
Photograph courtesy of Island Stone

FACING PAGE: Whether made of cut glass like the feather and paisley motifs, hand-glazed tiles like the tree of life, or waterjet-cut stone and glass like the gold-leafed Victor Horta-inspired design, a mosaic is the perfect starting point or finishing touch. The way the light reflects off of the small pieces yields a memorable kaleidoscope quality.
Photographs courtesy of New Ravenna, Artistic Tile and Metolius Ridge

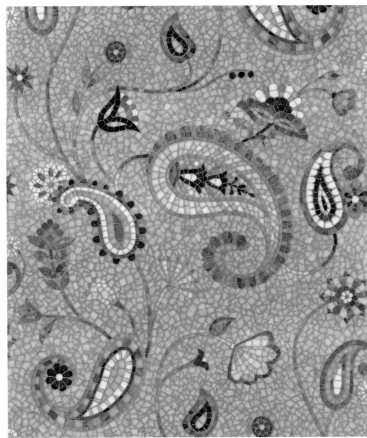

"The best part of this job is working with people to take a project from a concept to reality. Actually making something is very rewarding."

—Lee Hollowell

ABOVE: We obsess over the details. Because of this, discriminating architects, designers, and homeowners trust us with the most complex of projects. We can originate ideas and design the cabinetry, or we can execute the vision of the architect or designer. In any case, the project gets our undivided attention. The selection of hardware is often a critical element in the aesthetics of a piece or a room. This newly created Arts-and-Crafts-style cabinet has authenticity because of the custom, hammered copper hardware.
Photograph by Joe Martines

FACING PAGE: For the kitchen of a Bill Poss-designed seven-story mountainside home, we created cabinetry and paneling using plain-sliced birch and African padauk woods. Built-in furniture—beds, nightstands, dressers, desks—is a theme throughout the home, lending unity and simplicity to the look from room to room.
Photograph by Pat Sudmeier

"If you want to create with wood, you have to understand that wood moves and allow for it in your design."

—Joe Martines

LEFT: Walls, ceilings, beams, archways, columns—these are all more beautiful when finely crafted in wood. Raised paneling creates depth, shadows, and visual interest. These characteristics are appealing regardless of a home's style, and a limitless variety of finishes for wood makes this material suitable for any interior.
Photograph by Brent Moss

FACING PAGE TOP & BOTTOM RIGHT: The linen-fold paneling is inspired by English Gothic style. The process is painstaking—each panel is hand-carved in our workshop. For a true enthusiast of this English style, we paneled all four walls of a bedroom with this motif and designed and produced tables for the room. The quarter-sawn oak was hand-waxed to complete the authentic aesthetic of the room.
Top photograph by Brent Moss
Bottom right photograph by Joe Martines

FACING PAGE BOTTOM LEFT: The homeowner's request for Wild West style and plenty of storage was our inspiration for the figured mahogany bar with 14-inch crown moulding, curved glass, and intricate detailing. The piece is installed in a large riding arena attached to a private residence and serves its function admirably.
Photograph by Joe Martines

"High quality craftsmanship allows for no shortcuts. It is the sum of all the small details that creates the impression of the whole."

—Mark Bryan

ABOVE LEFT: The cherry beams and mouldings, coffered ceiling, paneling, and fireplace surround give the room solidity and authenticity. We designed and executed the millwork, working closely with the owners to achieve a pleasing solution to their needs.
Photograph by Brent Moss

ABOVE RIGHT: The project architect had a photo of what he had in mind. Using that as a starting point, we designed the one-piece balustrade with carved details. Staircases are complex projects that require careful attention in the design phase to avoid problems in the production and installation.
Photograph by Pat Sudmeier

FACING PAGE: You can do a lot with small spaces when imagination is given full rein. We transformed an old storage space into a cozy oak-paneled library. We had done other installations in the house and suggested this use, which was inspired by a picture clipped from a periodical. Our resulting design captured the spirit of this vision and fit with the existing interior of the house. Our workshop takes advantage of the newest technology available, both in the design and production areas, but we never stray from the principles of Old World craftsmanship.
Photograph by Brent Moss

MYERS & COMPANY ARCHITECTURAL METALS

Basalt, Colorado

"Nothing matches the raw beauty of Colorado like a fine work of architectural metal."

—Bob Myers

ABOVE & FACING PAGE: The owners' desire to stylistically complement the strength and beauty of the towering Douglas fir columns in their Snowmass home is portrayed in the abstract forgings of the branch railing design. The look and feel of the hand-chamfered silicon bronze hand railing was a natural choice to accompany the organic texture of the hand-forged iron and the warmth of the wood and stone entry.
Photographs by Ron Lloyd

ABOVE: An impressive gate draws attention to the mountain ranch home's entrance, which overlooks the Roaring Fork River Valley. Mimicking a steel bridge design, the gate's steel I-beam construction with its gusseted and through-bolted tubular steel posts is activated from a keypad entry and swings effortlessly on pivoting eight-inch-diameter steel columns.

FACING PAGE TOP: The free-span trellis is an extension of the Aspen mountain sanctuary's geometric forms and roof planes. Finished in a metallic coating, the 42-foot compound-angle tubular steel frame is a fully welded structure that casts welcome shade from the high summer sun and is engineered to support heavy mountain snows.

FACING PAGE BOTTOM: Exposed steel of a roof structure illustrates the amount of reinforcement that is needed in the mountains of Colorado. Roofs, especially with massive cantilevering, must be engineered to withstand the heavy weight of snow accumulation. The view just beyond includes the well-known ski trails of Snowmass.

Photographs by Ron Lloyd

"There are inherent challenges in working with metal, but the reward for patience and skill is a creation that will most certainly stand the test of time."

—Bob Myers

ABOVE: Though we design, engineer and install enormously complex architectural elements, we also design and create the softer, smaller interior design pieces that allow us to show off our whimsical, creative side.

FACING PAGE: Close collaboration resulted in the beautiful stairway for the Zwan family's Tuscan villa-style home in Aspen. The helical steel stair stringer is clad in Italian stone and supports the intricately forged iron balustrade with "cast on" steel post ornaments that are flush mounted at each step and finished off with a highly polished bronze cap railing.
Photographs by Ron Lloyd

CUSTOM EDGE MARBLE & GRANITE

Denver, Colorado

"Natural stone work is truly an art form."

—Jose Burciaga

ABOVE: For 18 years, we worked for one of the best natural stone fabrication companies around. But the demand for custom marble and granite was so great that we were able to open our own company, bringing together a team that can focus on providing the best quality. The custom design of this Juparana granite countertop is due to the reversed DuPont with cove edge detail.

FACING PAGE: The marble is Juparana Crema Bordeaux with a six-centimeter Ogee Edge Bullnose cut. Moving away from the standard edge individualizes the counter.
Photographs by Blanca S. Burciaga

"Detailing the edges brings out the natural beauty of the marble."

—Jose Burciaga

TOP LEFT: Smoothness and polishing are essential. The Pompeii granite, at three centimeters, gets an Ogee Edge Bullnose cut.

CENTER & BOTTOM LEFT: Juparana Crema Bordeaux is multifaceted. Wherever its placement may be, the edge completes the room. We pride ourselves on our ability to create any edge detail.

FACING PAGE: The edge details of the fireplace, as well as the design itself, were custom-made. The marble is honed Noce travertine, and our holistic process to develop the piece was as smooth as, well, the marble.
Photographs by Blanca S. Burciaga

"Creativity is the ability to look
beyond the obvious."

—Sara Zook

elements of design

chapter three

Sara Zook Designs offers an unmistakable look to its design projects. Drama, detail, and craftsmanship are brought to a new level with strong visual stimulation and perfect proportions. Combining creativity with more than 25 years of experience and national and international education, Sara Zook, ASID, approaches each project with an eclectic eye and flair for the unexpected. By listening to clients, Sara has mastered the art of interpretation. Owners get precisely the spaces they need, and so much more: designs that go beyond their expectations.

When working with homeowners, Sara believes that every home deserves great detailed spaces, comfort, and understated elegance, no matter the homeowner's style. Her diverse capabilities reveal everything from ultra-casual getaways to modern city dwellings—nothing is off limits. Her creative glasses never come off. Owning and operating two wholesale furniture lines, New Classics Creations and Beaumodern, Sara offers an array of benefits to homeowners. She can design the perfect piece for any room, whether it is furniture or a built-in element, to fit any personality, no matter how impossible it may seem. Access to a worldwide range of exotic veneers and inlays, as well as the most talented cabinet makers and carvers, gives her a clear advantage when designing and presents abilities and quality outside of the status quo. Her sweeping knowledge of furniture history and design philosophy manifests itself in spaces that are at once exciting, comforting, and casually elegant.

SARA ZOOK DESIGNS

"Embracing the diversity of design and refusing to focus on a single style opens up a world of possibilities."

—Sara Zook

RIGHT: When a city couple wanted to kick off their boots in their Colorado ranch home, we blended formal elements with casual country antiques, as though their family heirlooms had been brought by covered wagon. Designed to look like an aged log cabin, the space incorporates Queen Anne chairs and a spooled game table from New Classics, cashmere wool seating, a block plaid custom-braided wool rug, and the clients' exquisitely tooled saddles. Painted oxblood color floors and custom chandeliers made of fallow deer antlers and steel add to the welcoming ambience.
Photograph by Ron Ruscio

PREVIOUS PAGES: A custom three-story mahogany staircase with Art Deco rails serves as the graphic centerpiece of a downtown residence. The varied use of glass offers a strong, ethereal feel to the space, with glass treads, newel posts, mirrored consoles, and glass block walls.
Photograph by Todd Droy

"If the designer is not connected to the homeowner, the perceived boundaries for design and color are not stretched. Collaboration creates success."

—Sara Zook

ABOVE LEFT & RIGHT: A custom ebonized mahogany console sets the style in the entry of a stunning Denver home, while the dazzling appeal of a powder room beckons to be seen as a young yet graceful aesthetic. The delicate crystal chandelier and sconces contrast with a weathered trumeau mirror. The painted ironwork sink console in blue adds more color to the hand-screened blue and bronze wallpaper to complete the casual sophisticated mood.

FACING PAGE: An all-wooden walnut cupola bed by New Classics, with whorled posts, serves as the elegant focal point of a bedroom. Linen-upholstered walls, a French cowhide chair, and custom granite-topped consoles add to the refinement of the space.

Photographs by Ron Ruscio

ABOVE: A sitting room offers a cozy reading space off of an elegant bedroom with a down chaise, an inviting leather chair and ottoman, and a hand-made limestone fireplace with a limestone basket weave. Balloon shades detailed with rosettes add a soft touch to the space, while layers upon layers of color give depth to the hand-crafted Venetian plaster.
Photograph by Todd Droy

FACING PAGE TOP: Suede walls and leather-wrapped mouldings add layers of masculinity to a study for the gentleman of the house. Situated within a home in a world-class community, the study serves the need for both relaxation and international communication systems. Rich textures of cherry and yew make up the cabinets and desk, while wool draperies complete the ambience.
Photograph by Todd Droy

FACING PAGE BOTTOM: When designing a home for modern art collectors in a ski country log house, I knew that an eclectic look would be perfect. Chinese antiques, modern leather seating, an all-metal buffet, and a heavily distressed walnut table married with Windsor chairs give the spaces a collected, relaxed feel.
Photographs by Ron Ruscio

"Great fabrics and color are the backbone of a room."

—Sara Zook

TOP: For a music-loving family, an appropriate concert music room was imperative for gatherings. Careful consideration was given to the piano orientation and window design to allow for the perfect amount of daylight, illuminating the room. Elaborate draperies of aubergine and gold silk add to the festive ambience.
Photograph by Ron Ruscio

CENTER: A clean, modern look defines the living room. The thick wool Gabbeh rug, the modern leather sofas, and an antique chair upholstered in a flat-weave rug offer an array of textures.
Photograph by Todd Droy

BOTTOM: A North Shore Chicago home with a stunning stone fireplace shows off an international collection. Pillows, rugs, and primitive prints hail from France, Thailand, and a number of Eastern regions.
Photograph courtesy of Sara Zook Designs

FACING PAGE: My fireplace design blends beautifully with a 1690 French armoire replica featuring Jacobean-twist detailing. Cut-velvet draperies, a Gordon Brown painting, and rich hues of red and gold make the room irresistible.
Photograph by Todd Droy

"Interior design is as much about listening as it is about aesthetics."

—Sara Zook

RIGHT: A stainless steel fireplace blends with lightly shimmering, makore mahogany millwork and cabinetry from New Classics to create an international design style. Metallic sheers, a silk rug, and rich, deep hues of purple, plum, and gold make for lavish details. By using traditional materials in a non-traditional design, I created a modern space that will transcend time and showcase the homeowner's collections.
Photograph by Todd Droy

"Kitchens and baths are the most personal rooms of the home and, therefore, the design is identified by room behaviors based on human needs."

—Bev Adams

ABOVE & FACING PAGE: With the range hood as the focal point drawing you in, the built-in china buffet towers like a soldier, protecting the entrance and creating a boundary, balancing the length of this expansive 15-foot island that sits in the 20-foot kitchen. The subzero armoire is flanked by 42-inch countertops, allowing convenient access into the ovens housed in the base cabinetry. The countertop height change gives definition to the desk, which is an invaluable resource for a mother of sporting enthusiasts. The rich texture of each quadrant is repeated throughout as seen in the stone inlays of the subzero cabinet, base entry cabinet, island, and range hood.
Photographs by Jason Young

"While I make a point to include the time-honored triangle in each kitchen, it is the healing power of the design elements in the kitchen that plays a vital role in creating the space."

—Bev Adams

ABOVE & FACING PAGE: Setting foot in this kitchen is an unforgettable experience. The space is saturated in texture and designed in the shape of a cross with intersecting lines. This offers the functionality of two separate kitchens in one cohesive space. One island creates a sense of mystery while the other shows off its large stature. Like puzzle pieces, the countertops fit together in harmony of positive and negative space. The glass cabinets represent windows, creating the illusion that you can see through to the other side.
Photographs by Ron Ruscio

ABOVE: The importance of balance cannot be overstated. I'm inspired by the words of John Ruskin, "When love and skill work together, expect a masterpiece." Through my unique approach to interior space planning, all of my designs embody that creative spirit.

FACING PAGE: I crafted the space from scratch combining sections of the furniture line from Habersham to create an exquisite design. Various textures, including dramatic woods and subtly veined granite, are combined for brilliant effect.

Photographs by Ron Ruscio

"The kitchen is an area of congregation and celebration where secrets are exchanged, guests are welcomed, and memories are created and displayed."

—Bev Adams

LEFT: In order to continually recall the sentiment of the couple's European travel experiences, I designed the kitchen with lavish detail and ornate architectural embellishment. The look and feel of this regal, Old-World cabinetry inspires a strong Baroque influence, yet it maintains a convenient, high-tech functionality.
Photograph by Ron Ruscio

"I approach space planning and design with an emphasis on the psychology of the space and how it will be used, in conjunction with the wants and needs of the people who will use it."

—Bev Adams

LEFT & FACING PAGE: In a home that is constantly full of family and friends, the movement between the countertops is fluid, natural, easily accessible. The octagonal design features a variety of heights and depths for ease of use; each of the island's sides is a different length to maximize workspace. Facing walls have symmetrical counters, ledges, and spaces, creating an aura of peace and tranquility. Every wall has a unique design story, and every design element is intentional.
Photographs by Ron Ruscio

"It's very important to specify the right products and finishes for each space and the people who will interact with it. The impact is a reflection of the homeowners' lifestyle and personality."

—Bev Adams

ABOVE & FACING PAGE: I helped an aviation enthusiast incorporate his passion into his kitchen. The back of the island is clad in material resembling the belly of an airplane; extensions of the room simulate the look and feel of a jet wing. The tall bar cabinetry sits at the end of the kitchen with full capacity for serving a large group. Using a minimalist approach while maintaining warmth, we used four main elements for the interior: glass, solid cherry, stainless steel, and makore veneer. These alternating textures appear throughout, creating interest and stimulation.

Photographs by Ron Ruscio

"Design means making the impossible look simple."

—Greg Phare

ABOVE: When an interior designer wanted to include a mechanical element in the design of an audio visual installation, we used symmetry as an art piece and allowed some of the more technical elements to come through. The DVD player, cable box, amplifiers, cooling system, personal computer, and DVD manager are visible on either side of the screen while the speakers hide behind transparent audio cloth.

FACING PAGE: Staying in sync with the architecture of the home allows us to create nearly invisible installations. As a result, spaces remain clean and elegant with few hints of the extensive home automation system. Lutron shading with a custom-made valance offers a contemporary, sleek look to the space, while minimal clues give away the complex, energy efficient system at play. HVAC, whole-house speaker system, lighting, and shading are managed by two control points: a user-friendly remote and a simple touch panel.

Photographs courtesy of Digital Media Innovations

"What you don't see is just as important as what you do. Whether it's a comprehensive security system or basic climate control, there's always more than meets the eye."

—Greg Phare

ABOVE: Our clean, elegant installation in a loft bedroom offers the best of both worlds. The dual-shading system has a sheer shade option that gives privacy to the homeowners while providing sunlight; the blackout shade allows for complete darkness. Customized acoustical material adds a distinct, soft-paneled look that the designer wanted for the space.

FACING PAGE TOP: The mechanical aspect of our work is obviously important; but we don't sacrifice the aesthetics of a room. Because controlling the ambience was a priority for a large living room, we created a full Lutron lighting system with electronic shades—the shading system reduced heat issues as well as HVAC costs. Encased in a flush-mount pocket, the three large windows serve as the room's focal point and provide as much or as little light as the occasion requires.

FACING PAGE BOTTOM: Our flexibility and creativity make anything possible. Retrofitting a turn-of-the-century home required both ingenuity and careful preservation. We built a pop-up plasma lift in a replica of an Old World furniture piece, achieving modern luxury without forfeiting the integrity of the home's style. And for the kitchen, we built a corner unit that blends seamlessly with the room while providing an audio visual element that the homeowner requested. *Photographs courtesy of Digital Media Innovations*

"It isn't all about technology and mechanics; aesthetics play a critical role in a system's design."

—Greg Phare

ABOVE: As we retrofitted a contemporary loft, we included Lutron dimmers and custom-metal window work. We also took creative measures to design the perfect shading. Our installations match the home's style, blending with the architectural elements of the space; exposed concrete and ceilings offer an edgy, industrial look.

FACING PAGE: Undoubtedly clean and sleek, a home office space shows off the benefits of wireless technology and smart design. Office automation turns board rooms, conference rooms, and offices into top-of-the-line work spaces. We also design computer networks, giving us the ability to fully incorporate and understand what an office—home or commercial—needs for success.
Photographs courtesy of Digital Media Innovations

"From 2,400° F molten glass we cast thick, deeply carved glass plates for windows, doors, and more."

—Jacqueline Spiro

ABOVE: For a condominium kitchen high above Las Vegas, Nevada, we created a glass countertop with a contemporary Aspen leaf motif. Suspended over polished granite, the glass provides infinitely varying reflections of life above the storied city.
Photograph by Britt Pierson

FACING PAGE: The floral design carved into the glass entry doors emulates their setting high in the Rockies. The glass is poured into hardened sandstone-like molds made of fine sand and resin. Designs are then hand carved into the molds using high speed diamond tools. The carving often protrudes as much as an inch from the base glass.
Photograph by Dave Marlow

ABOVE: Glass inserts and an architect's design turn a porte cochère entryway into art. The massive door opens around a central pivot point. For the openings in this thick door, two glass sections—one for the interior and one for the exterior—come together in each hole. We used three color variations for added interest. The sidelights of glass display designs in extremely high relief.
Photograph by Jason Dewey

FACING PAGE: We use wood and steel with our glass to fashion distinctive furniture. The nesting tables use both clear and green colored glass. We also do sculptural pieces for clients and galleries.
Photographs by Dave Marlow

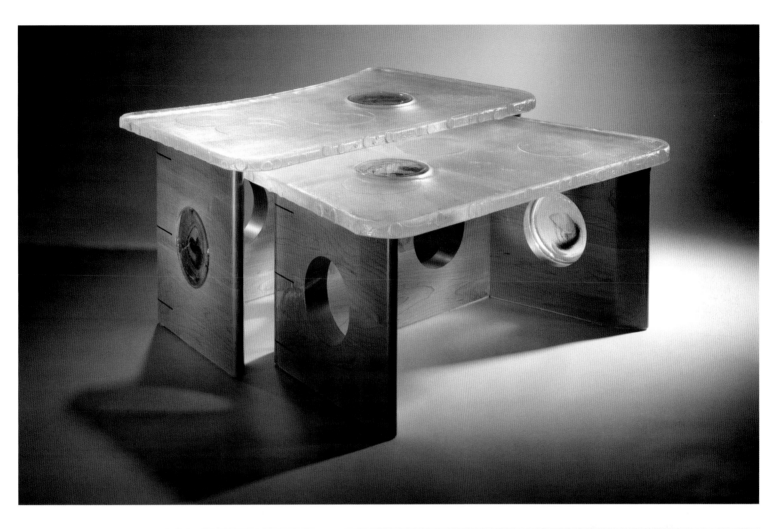

"Most of our glass is well over one inch thick. It invites the viewers to run their fingers over it."

—Lee Lyon

ABOVE & FACING PAGE: The owners of an Iowa lake home wanted to differentiate the entry area from their large living area without reducing the light in either space. Working closely with them, we designed a 22-foot-long, nine-foot-high freestanding sculptural wall. The final design invites visitors to linger a bit before moving into the main room. A couple of wood shelves pass through the wall, allowing for functional displays on special occasions.
Photographs by Di Hirt

BOB LEVEY DECORATIVE FINISHING

Basalt, Colorado

"Old World painting techniques bring classic European style into the modern era."

—Bob Levey

ABOVE: For hundreds of years, people have tried to mimic natural materials in order to expand design possibilities. High-end, decorative wood finishing is a highly complicated design choice that, when done correctly, appears simple, giving the essence of the timeless European tradition. The home, with architecture by Bill Poss and interior architecture by Arthur Chabon, shows some of the design possibilities in wood finishing.
Photograph by Joel Eden

FACING PAGE: The patina of wood runs throughout the house, achieving an Old World elegance. The home was designed by Bill Poss.
Photograph by Pat Sudmeier

"A lot of work goes into making something simple."

—Bob Levey

TOP: The decorative applications of faux marble and wood graining are endless. With design by Jean Luis Deniot and Irish Gorman, the Aspen project has an ambience that radiates from the wood finishing.

CENTER: The home features a faux marble chinoiserie, a relief that is raised for dimension and hand-painted to give a painterly, artistic sensibility.

BOTTOM: Some faux-marble pieces reveal the depth of what many years of experience can produce.

FACING PAGE: A long history of wood-graining tradition has opened the doors to new possibilities in home design. I've always tried to achieve the highest level of design and balance.
Photographs by Joel Eden

"With glass, precision can make or, literally, break a project."

—David Uhey

ABOVE LEFT: Twenty years ago, when we started, glass companies didn't want to touch frameless shower doors. There was a large demand for this product and other high-end, custom-fabricated glass installations. DGI was founded with this market in mind. A glass shower and sink/countertop combination offers an ultra-contemporary look that remains in vogue today.

ABOVE RIGHT: Artists hand cut and sandblast designs into glass for an ideal, one-of-a-kind shower door.

FACING PAGE: At a mountain home, we created a glass-railing system to offer a unique, highly customized design. We had to figure out how to stabilize the glass panels, attaching them at the sides of the second-story floor with metal fixtures. Precision was everything.
Photographs courtesy of Denver Glass Interiors

"It's intricate work, but designing in-house individualizes every project."

—David Uhey

ABOVE LEFT: To make a bold statement, cast glass can be used in frameless shower doors. Artisans shape a mold and press heated glass into it. The result is beautiful.

ABOVE CENTER: As a backdrop to an office reception area, cast glass offers an artistic touch, here strung with heavy-duty cabling.

ABOVE RIGHT: Clean, contemporary frameless shower glass with curves! These glass creations are architectural elements that invigorate the home. We acquired the best Italian-made glass fabrication equipment and a tempering oven to produce over 90 percent of the glass we install in our shop. Our large, elegant showrooms give people a chance to touch and feel samples, to open and close doors, to get a good sense of their options.

FACING PAGE: In a high-rise loft in downtown Denver, a glass railing gives a very contemporary aesthetic. With glass treads running upward, the stairway answers the need for high-end glass, a need for which we have traveled the country to fulfill.
Photographs courtesy of Denver Glass Interiors

GALLEGOS CORPORATION

Vail, Colorado — Aspen, Colorado — Denver, Colorado — Sun Valley, Idaho

"Stone appeals to the senses—it is strong and powerful."

—Gary Woodworth

ABOVE: With the appearance of seamlessness, the custom-fabricated 14-foot-long radius-front marble vanity with integral sinks and backsplash was created from Giallo Reale marble. We fashioned it from slabs to yield a final appearance of a solid block structure.

FACING PAGE: We outfitted a mountain contemporary home with a two-sided fireplace that brings together warm colors, texture, and clean lines. Ashlar veneer is paired with a Mariana soapstone cantilevered hearth for diversity.
Photographs by Todd Winslow Pierce

"The beauty of stone can transform a home."

—Gerald Gallegos

ABOVE: The idea of the remodel was to bring the family room to the kitchen. The fireplace was added, and the room was opened to include the living area in the home's most popular room. A stone fireplace, plaster walls and ceilings, granite countertops, and stone floors were all introduced.

FACING PAGE TOP LEFT: A castle-like game and wine-tasting room was created in the basement level of a home where the family frequently entertains. Stone floors, walls, and ceilings meet blue Venetian plaster accent walls, which match the felt on the family's billiards table.

FACING PAGE TOP RIGHT: The home is situated in a grove of aspen trees. The owners wanted to feel as though they were at a spa while enjoying their steam shower. The bath was redesigned to bring the outside in. We used a vertically oriented glass-mosaic wall tile, and one-by-one-inch glass tile at the shower floor and ceiling. Honed granite wall elements, a corner shelving unit, niche, and bench take the room one step further.

FACING PAGE BOTTOM LEFT: A single piece of carved onyx was used to create the beautiful lines present. Soft green plaster walls accent the veins in the white onyx.

FACING PAGE BOTTOM RIGHT: The homeowners provided the cast stone fireplace for our team to install. They wanted a raised hearth, but it was not available from the cast stone supplier. We fabricated the radius-front limestone to complement the homeowners' fireplace surround.
Photographs by Todd Winslow Pierce

"Recreating nature is the ultimate challenge and an art form in itself."

—Scott Sones

living the elements

chapter four

Residential landscape architecture is not merely the design of plantings. It is equally, if not more so, the planning of the outdoor living spaces. Simple questions reveal so much. How will the owners use the outdoor space? How do we complement the home's architectural style? Once these answers become clear, a well-planned approach comes together, and the elements fall into place.

Working closely with the architect and the residents, Scott Sones and Jamie McCluskie craft outdoor living spaces that serve as extensions of the home. The success of their collaboration through SonesMac Landscape Architecture led to the establishment of Sones Landscape Architecture Group and MacDesign, two firms with distinct focuses and the talent and experience to undertake even the most complex of projects. Colorado's unique topography presents itself as a continual challenge, sparking innovative design solutions that lead to the most stunning outdoor settings. Scott and Jamie have unsurpassed knowledge of Western plant life, giving them an extraordinary database from which to draw inspiration. They often incorporate native grasses and indigenous plants to enhance a home's natural surroundings and hold preserving the site and its views as a top priority—a guideline that steers every design.

SONES LANDSCAPE ARCHITECTURE GROUP AND MACDESIGN

"It's important to carefully consider the climate when choosing a plant palette. Colorado demands hearty varieties that withstand our heavy snow and higher elevations."

—Scott Sones

RIGHT & PREVIOUS PAGES: The outdoor leisure space is naturally set and carved within massive boulder groupings—some as large as 12 feet in diameter—incorporating water features, art pieces, an architectural bridge, and flowing drifts of ornamental grasses and perennial flowers. Built elements nod to the mountain vernacular of the home, while plant life harmoniously integrates with existing natural features. We complemented mature cottonwoods that line the lake with a few ponderosa pines. The scene is carefully framed from every vantage point to ensure a natural feel. Design by Scott Sones.
Photographs courtesy of SonesMac

"The transition from the manmade elements to the existing native environment must be overlapping, creating a seamless integration."

—Scott Sones

ABOVE: We utilized a natural water source that flows through the property at nearly six cubic feet per second. The stream enters the site as a dramatic waterfall at the entry court, carving its way through the site and forming a series of ponds that create a mirrored foreground to the spectacular mountain views beyond. The waterwheel adds a historic element to the mountain home.

FACING PAGE TOP: Because of the cool climate, we had to ensure that the pool could be outfitted with an automatic cover. Therefore, we went with a traditional rectangular form and designed the space to it. When we incorporate a body of water that is intended to look manmade, we have to conscientiously blend it into the site; the further you get from the house and toward the forested area, the more natural the landscape design comes across.

FACING PAGE BOTTOM: The 25-foot water element makes for a tranquil arrival experience. Perennials and aspens bring the forest vibe to the architecture. Designs by Scott Sones.
Photographs courtesy of SonesMac

ABOVE: Designs with natural boulders can't exactly be sketched out on paper. You have a rough idea of how many stones you'll need and what sizes will work best, but the real art happens when you're physically putting the composition together. In collaboration with a landscape contractor and a notable water-feature builder, we worked to create a natural aesthetic with the flow of the stream and placement of boulders and aquatic plantings. The plantings are a challenge as the gravel and soil pockets have to be carefully integrated with the waterproof liner. The efforts, however, are the finishing details that provide the timeless look.

FACING PAGE: The alpine courtyard is an eloquent response to the Colorado lifestyle. The art mirror reflects light to the shady space and adds a curious interest. Designs by Scott Sones.
Photographs courtesy of SonesMac

"The most successful plantings are dictated by the site's natural elements."

—Jamie McCluskie

ABOVE: Inspired by the architecture, the garden wall niches have operable wooden windows that allow extra light and gentle breezes to flow through the garden. Flagstone pavers serve as an eroded extension of the formal terrace and create a memorable garden experience. Design by Scott Sones.

FACING PAGE TOP: Mature trees are a wonderful backdrop for casual outdoor entertainment spaces. Design by Jamie McCluskie.

FACING PAGE BOTTOM: The boulder artwork and textural native grasses are distinctively Colorado. Design by Scott Sones.
Photographs courtesy of SonesMac

ABOVE, LEFT, & FACING PAGE: Landscape design is a subject that can be learned in school, but it's really more of an intuitive practice. Inspiration comes from the beauty of the mountains, the uniqueness of each site, the distinct qualities of the architecture, and a lifetime of visual experiences. I opt for sustainable design elements such as geothermal heating when possible and believe that the best designs are those that tread lightly on the earth and feel as if they've always been in their place. Whether I'm bringing a little bit of Cape Cod to the Rockies or helping to smooth the transition between a contemporary home and nature, I take an organic, integrated approach. Design by Scott Sones.
Photographs courtesy of SonesMac

BLUEGREEN

Aspen, Colorado

"Great landscape architecture balances environmental stewardship with exceptional design aesthetic."

—Valerie Alexander Yaw

ABOVE: Since its beginning, Bluegreen has sought to explore modern landscape design, intimately intertwined with sustainability. All of the projects begin here. An outdoor room is created with a planting bed tipped at an angle, layered plantings, and a rammed earth wall, all of which ensure privacy and enclosure while screening views of neighboring residences.

FACING PAGE: The integration of fire, water, and earth creates three distinct rooms—a striking autocourt, a contemplative Zen water garden, and a minimalist terrace. Here, the south-facing entertaining terrace utilizes passive heating and cooling techniques to extend its use into three seasons. Architecture by Studio B.
Photographs by Jason Dewey/Bluegreen

"Inventive, thoughtful and responsive landscape design allows architecture to have interesting exterior living spaces and truly creates a lifestyle experience."

—Bill Poss

ABOVE: Site preservation and maintaining existing, healthy ecosystems are among the most effective ways to achieve a sustainable landscape and are inherently cost-effective as well. The residence is situated in a unique stand of mature ponderosa pines that required careful preservation. Here, a seamless transition to native landscape is made while creating terraces and sitting areas. By incorporating fire-wise strategies into the design, we created defensible spaces between the residence and native landscape in high wildfire hazard conditions.

FACING PAGE TOP: The created stream brings nature into the residence. The stream collects and conveys stormwater and provides a closer visual and aural connection to the pond located below the residence. At one point the stream opens to a shallow pool and brushes the architecture so closely one can reach out and touch it.

FACING PAGE BOTTOM: The stainless-steel rods are Bluegreen envisioned and designed—lightheartedly referred to as "pokey poles." At the spa, the stainless-steel rods, varying in height, become landscape art and double as a place to hang one's robe. Playful and functional, the poles individually mimic the trees of the adjacent grove and their varying heights. Viewed as a whole, the poles mimic the mountainous skyline. Invisibly integrated, some of the poles are modified to be light fixtures and illuminate the path to the spa. Architecture by Poss Architecture + Planning.

Photographs by Jason Dewey/Bluegreen

ABOVE: The homeowners enjoy entertaining and an upbeat family life, and their pool and well-planned, generous terrace suit them perfectly. A spare, minimalist design with a restrained palette of materials reinterprets the dark mountain pond with sandy beach. The stream meanders down to the pond—or in this case, a modern pool. The essence of the project is captured in this composition where all things social occur.

LEFT: Stream water shows playfulness and beauty as it spills, slips, and disappears between plinths of stone. The layered materials and abstract elements reinforce the graphic modern interpretation of a mountain stream when viewed from above.

FACING PAGE: Controlled design is reinforced through repetition of the minimal materials palette. The division of indoors and out is blurred, and the hardscape takes its theme from the mountain stream and pond, with floating stones providing crossing of the cobble stream. The landscape exemplifies Bluegreen's philosophy of timelessness and transparency in the design work. Architecture by Stone Fox, water feature by Water + Stone, and general construction by Brikor Associates.
Photographs by Jason Dewey/Bluegreen and Travis Fulton

GALLEGOS CORPORATION

Vail, Colorado — Aspen, Colorado — Denver, Colorado — Sun Valley, Idaho

"The diversity of stone is so large, expertise in the subject is the best solution."

—Sam Johnson

ABOVE: Fire and water drive the design of a flat streamside area, which the family wanted to transform into an outdoor living area. The fire pit keeps the coolness of the water from overpowering the owners, allowing more time to enjoy the tranquility of the rushing stream.

FACING PAGE: Stone paving, treads, veneer, and copings can transform an outdoor space. Curves soften the stone, and the varying heights of the stone decks create separate outdoor spaces. The rusty brown colors of the stone veneer are carried into the paving, with the solid color of the treads, caps, and copings used to highlight design aspects.
Photographs by Todd Winslow Pierce

"You can't build anything without integrity."

—Gary Woodworth

ABOVE: Water flows smoothly across the negative edge of the pool. The rough stone veneer creates contrast with the dimensional black granite at the water feature.
Photograph by Steve Mundinger

FACING PAGE TOP LEFT: The owner desired a soft linear look for the veneer, so the stone was lightly tumbled to round the edges and smooth the face. Punched openings in the enclosed patio wall offer an Old World appeal.
Photograph by Harris Photo Graphic

FACING PAGE TOP RIGHT: The stepping of the stone patios and site walls keeps the change in elevation to a human scale, avoiding the impression of a deep canyon while preserving the owners' privacy.
Photograph by Todd Winslow Pierce

FACING PAGE BOTTOM LEFT: The owner wanted a patio with a fire pit that could be enjoyed year-round. The heated patio surrounding the fire pit adds to the warmth of the fire.
Photograph by Todd Winslow Pierce

FACING PAGE BOTTOM RIGHT: The arched stone bridge and meandering stone path lead to several patios with distinct landscape elements at each patio.
Photograph by Todd Winslow Pierce

perspectives
ON DESIGN

COLORADO TEAM

SENIOR ASSOCIATE PUBLISHER: Karla Setser

GRAPHIC DESIGNER: Ashley DuPree

EDITOR: Daniel Reid

MANAGING PRODUCTION COORDINATOR: Kristy Randall

HEADQUARTERS TEAM

PUBLISHER: Brian G. Carabet

PUBLISHER: John A. Shand

EXECUTIVE PUBLISHER: Phil Reavis

DIRECTOR OF DEVELOPMENT & DESIGN: Beth Benton Buckley

PUBLICATION & CIRCULATION MANAGER: Lauren B. Castelli

SENIOR GRAPHIC DESIGNER: Emily A. Kattan

GRAPHIC DESIGNER: Kendall Muellner

MANAGING EDITOR: Rosalie Z. Wilson

EDITOR: Anita M. Kasmar

EDITOR: Michael McConnell

EDITOR: Jennifer Nelson

EDITOR: Sarah Tangney

EDITOR: Lindsey Wilson

PRODUCTION COORDINATOR: Maylin Medina

PRODUCTION COORDINATOR: Drea Williams

TRAFFIC COORDINATOR: Brandi Breaux

ADMINISTRATIVE MANAGER: Carol Kendall

ADMINISTRATIVE ASSISTANT: Beverly Smith

CLIENT SUPPORT COORDINATOR: Amanda Mathers

PANACHE PARTNERS, LLC

CORPORATE HEADQUARTERS

1424 Gables Court

Plano, TX 75075

469.246.6060

www.panache.com

www.panachedesign.com

index

Bluegreen 179
Sheri Sanzone, ASLA, AICP, LEED AP
Valerie Alexander Yaw, ASLA, LEED AP
300 South Spring Street, Suite 202
Aspen, CO 81611
970.429.7499
www.bluegreenaspen.com

Bob Levey Decorative Finishing 155
Bob Levey
0031 Duroux Lane, Unit C
Basalt, CO 81621
970.927.5009
www.boblevey.net

Brikor Associates 19
Briston Peterson
Korba Andrews
PO Box 1361
Aspen, CO 81612
970.923.3088
www.brikor.com

Brown Dog Designs 103
Lee Hollowell
Joe Martines
Mark Bryan
0394 Crystal Circle
Carbondale, CO 81623
970.963.1924
www.browndogdesignsinc.com

Custom Edge Marble & Granite 115
Jose Burciaga
710 Umatilla
Denver, CO 80204
303.825.0141
www.customedgedenver.com

Decorative Materials International 91
Margot Hampleman
595 South Broadway, Suite 121E
Denver, CO 80209
303.722.1333
150 Basalt Center Circle
Basalt, CO 81621
970.927.0700
105 Edwards Village Boulevard, Suite A204
Edwards, CO 81632
970.926.2322
www.decorativematerials.com

Denver Glass Interiors 159
David Uhey
1600 West Evans Avenue
Englewood, CO 80110
303.744.0350
815 Ten Mile Drive
Frisco, CO 80443
970.668.8866
www.denverglassinteriors.com

Digital Media Innovations 143
Greg Phare
3065 South Broadway
Englewood, CO 80113
303.873.1100
www.digitalmediainnovations.com

Gallegos Corporation 163, 185
Dave Little
PO Box 821
Vail, CO 81658
970.926.3737
www.gallegoscorp.com

Harrison Custom Builders, Ltd. 29
Lynn Harrison
Pam Harrison
Scott Harrison
Christie Harrison
Rod Harrison
1500 West Thomas Avenue
Englewood, CO 80110
303.905.0229
303.471.9543
www.harrisoncustombuilders.com

In-Site Design Group 79
Judy Gubner, ASID, CAPS
Colleen Johnson, ASID, CAPS
1280 South Clayton Street
Denver, CO 80210
303.691.9000
www.insite-design-group.com

Interior Intuitions 131
Bev Adams
288 Clayton Street, Suite 100
Denver, CO 80206
303.355.2772
www.interiorintuitions.com

K.H. Webb Architects 39
Kyle Webb
710 West Lionshead Circle, Unit A
Vail, CO 81657
970.477.2990
www.khwebb.com

MacDesign 167
Jamie McCluskie
PO Box 6446
Avon, CO 81620
970.513.9345

**Myers & Company
Architectural Metals** 109
Bob Myers
555 Basalt Avenue
Basalt, CO 81621
970.927.4761
www.myersandco.com

Pinnacle Mountain Homes 49
Chris Renner
PO Box 1390
Breckenridge, CO 80424
970.453.0727
www.pinnaclemtnhomes.com

Poss Architecture + Planning 59
Bill Poss
605 East Main Street
Aspen, CO 81611
970.925.4755
www.billposs.com

Sara Zook Designs 119
Sara Zook, ASID
3700 Havana Street, Suite 301
Denver, CO 80239
303.237.4544
www.sarazookdesigns.com

Sears Barrett Architects .69
Sears Barrett
7901 East Belleview Avenue, Suite 250
Englewood, CO 80111
303.804.0688
www.searsbarrett.com

Sones Landscape Architecture Group 167
Scott Sones
PO Box 115
Avon, CO 81620
970.949.3286
www.sonesla.com

Spiro Lyon Glass 149
Jacqueline Spiro
Lee Lyon
17283 Highway 82
Carbondale, CO 81623
970.274.1192
www.spirolyonglass.com

THE PANACHE COLLECTION

CREATING SPECTACULAR PUBLICATIONS FOR DISCERNING READERS

Dream Homes Series
An Exclusive Showcase of the Finest Architects, Designers and Builders

Carolinas	*Northern California*
Chicago	*Ohio & Pennsylvania*
Coastal California	*Pacific Northwest*
Colorado	*Philadelphia*
Deserts	*South Florida*
Florida	*Southwest*
Georgia	*Tennessee*
Los Angeles	*Texas*
Metro New York	*Washington, D.C.*
Michigan	
Minnesota	
New England	
New Jersey	

Spectacular Homes Series
An Exclusive Showcase of the Finest Interior Designers

California	*New York*
Carolinas	*Ohio & Pennsylvania*
Chicago	*Pacific Northwest*
Colorado	*Philadelphia*
Florida	*South Florida*
Georgia	*Southwest*
Heartland	*Tennessee*
London	*Texas*
Michigan	*Toronto*
Minnesota	*Washington, D.C.*
New England	*Western Canada*

Perspectives on Design Series
Design Philosophies Expressed by Leading Professionals

California	*Great Lakes*
Carolinas	*Minnesota*
Chicago	*New England*
Colorado	*Pacific Northwest*
Florida	*Southwest*
Georgia	

Art of Celebration Series
The Making of a Gala

Chicago
Georgia
Midwest
New York
Philadelphia
South Florida
Southern California
Southwest
Texas
Washington, D.C.
Wine Country

Spectacular Wineries Series
A Captivating Tour of Established, Estate and Boutique Wineries

California's Central Coast
Napa Valley
New York
Sonoma County

Specialty Titles
The Finest in Unique Luxury Lifestyle Publications

Cloth and Culture: Ruth E. Funk
Distinguished Inns of North America
Extraordinary Homes California
Geoffrey Bradfield Ex Arte
Into the Earth: A Wine Cave Renaissance
Spectacular Golf of Colorado
Spectacular Golf of Texas
Spectacular Hotels
Spectacular Restaurants of Texas
Visions of Design

City by Design Series
An Architectural Perspective

Atlanta
Charlotte
Chicago
Dallas
Denver
Orlando
Phoenix
San Francisco
Texas

PanacheDesign.com
Where the Design Industry's Finest Professionals Gather, Share, and Inspire

PANACHE **design**

PanacheDesign.com overflows with innovative ideas from leading architects, builders, interior designers, and other specialists. A gallery of design photographs and library of advice-oriented articles are among the comprehensive site's offerings.

PANACHE PARTNERS, LLC • 1424 GABLES COURT • PLANO, TEXAS 75075 • 469.246.6060 • WWW.PANACHE.COM